D1127992

Little Pebble™

What Are Thunderstorms?

by Mari Schuh

PEBBLE
a capstone imprint

Little Pebble is published by Pebble
1710 Roe Crest Drive,
North Mankato, Minnesota 56003
www.mycapstone.com

Library of Congress Cataloging-in-Publication Data
Names: Schuh, Mari C., 1975–author.
Title: What are thunderstorms? / by Mari Schuh.
Description: North Mankato, Minnesota : Pebble, a Capstone imprint, [2019] Series: Little pebble. Wicked weather | Audience: Ages 4–8.
Identifiers: LCCN 2018029837 (print) | LCCN 2018031696 (ebook) | ISBN 9781977103376 (eBook PDF) | ISBN 9781977103307 (hardcover) | ISBN 9781977105479 (paperback)
Subjects: LCSH: Thunderstorms—Juvenile literature.
Classification: LCC QC968.2 (ebook) | LCC QC968.2 .S38 2019 (print) | DDC 551.55/4—dc23
LC record available at https://lccn.loc.gov/2018029837

Editorial Credits
Nikki Potts, editor; Kyle Grenz, designer;
Heather Mauldin, media researcher; Tori Abraham, production specialist

Photo Credits
Getty Images: William Anderson, 17; iStockphoto: JenniferPhotographyImaging, 11, mdesigner125, 9; Shutterstock: Irina Kozorog, 19, Jeff Gammons StormVisuals, 1, 7, John D Sirlin, cover, 21, Viktor Gladkov, 13, yevgeniy11, 5

Printed and bound in China.
000966

Table of Contents

What Is a Thunderstorm?

See the lightning.

It flashes bright in the sky.

Then boom!

It thunders.

A thunderstorm is here!

A thunderstorm is

a rain storm.

It has thick, dark clouds.

Watch out!

A strong wind blows.

It knocks down trees.

Lots of rain falls.

Watch out for a flash flood.

Look!

Hail falls.

It can be as big as a golf ball.

Hail can hurt cars and houses.

hail

Staying Safe

Lightning hits tall objects. Stay away from trees and towers.

NEW
YORKER

Go inside.

It is safer there.

You will be dry too.

Some storms last six hours.

Be safe!

Glossary

flash flood—a flood that happens with little or no warning, often during periods of heavy rainfall

hail—small balls of ice that form in thunderstorm clouds; hail falls from the sky

lightning—the electricity caused by friction in a cloud

safe—free from harm

thunder—the loud, rumbling sound that comes after lightning

thunderstorm—a rain storm with thunder and lightning

tower—a tall structure or building or a part of a building

Read More

Cox Cannons, Helen. *Thunder and Lightning.* Weather Wise. Chicago: Heinemann Library, 2015.

Fretland VanVoorst, Jenny. *Lightning.* Weather Watch. Minneapolis: Bullfrog Books, 2017.

Jensen, Belinda. *A Party for Clouds: Thunderstorms.* Bel the Weather Girl. Minneapolis: Millbrook Press, 2016.

Internet Sites

Use FactHound to find Internet sites related to this book.

Visit www.facthound.com

Just type in 9781977103307 and go.

Check out projects, games and lots more at **www.capstonekids.com**

Critical Thinking Questions

1. What do you hear during a thunderstorm? What do you see?
2. Name one way you can stay safe during a thunderstorm.
3. What falls from the sky during a thunderstorm?

Index